SEASONAL JOKES AND RIDDLES

Christmas & New Year Special

This book belongs to:

____

____

ABOUT KODE SCRIPT

Welcome to Kode Script, a dynamic publishing company dedicated to crafting digital stories with precision.

At Kode Script, we believe in the transformative power of creativity and education. Specializing in a diverse range of publications, from enchanting coloring books that spark imagination to mind-teasing riddles and puzzles for all ages, we cater to children, adults, and senior individuals alike.

Our mission is to seamlessly blend entertainment with learning, providing enriching experiences through meticulously designed content. With a commitment to quality and innovation, Kode Script invites you to embark on a journey where every page tells a story, and every puzzle unveils a new adventure.

If you like our books, please provide your positive reviews on Amazon or any other marketplace. your support will motivate us to do better.

 email : info@kodescript.com    www.kodescript.com

COPYRIGHT© 2024 BY KODE SCRIPT
ALL RIGHTS RESERVED

Why was the Christmas tree so bad at sewing?
Because it always dropped its needles!

What do you call a greedy elf?
Elfish.

Why doesn't Santa use GPS?
He follows the 'star' directions!

What's a snowman's favorite drink?
Iced tea.

How does a snowman get around?
By riding an 'icicle'

Why did the elf go to school?
To improve his 'elf'-esteem.

What do you get when you cross a
snowman with a dog?
Frostbite.

What kind of photos do elves take?
Elfies.

Why was the candy cane so quiet?
Because it was 'mint' to be.

How does Rudolph know when Christmas is coming?
He checks his 'calen-deer.'

Why was the clock excited for New Year's Eve?
It was ready to have a ball.

What do you call a ghost's New Year's party?
Boo Year's Eve.

Why don't calendars ever get tired?
They're always refreshed every year.

What's a bee's favorite way to celebrate New Year's Eve?
With a buzz!

Why don't you argue with New Year's resolutions?
They always seem right on time.

What did the champagne glass say to the bottle?
You pop my cork!

Why do people plant flowers on New Year's Day?
For fresh beginnings.

What did the New Year's toast say to the butter?
Let's start this year on a roll!

What's the most predictable New Year's resolution?
1080p vision.

Why did the fireworks blush?
They saw the spark between two people.

What do you call a New Year's resolution kept for one day?
A January Fools' joke.

Why did the chef host a New Year's Eve party?
To stir up some fun!

What's a New Year's baby's favorite sport?
Kick-off.

Why was the elevator excited for New Year's?
It wanted to go up in the world.

What's the best way to say goodbye
to the old year?

With a toast and a tear.

Why do gym memberships increase in
January?

**It's the perfect time to "work out"
old habits.**

Why did the clock stop at midnight on
New Year's?

**It wanted to be on time for the big
moment.**

What do cows say on New Year's
Eve?
Moo Year!

Why do phones love New Year's?
**They get a fresh start with new
resolutions.**

What's a vampire's favorite New
Year's tradition?
Counting down.

Why did the traffic light host a party?
It wanted to turn over a new light.

What's a cat's New Year's resolution?
Purr more, hiss less.

What did the balloon say on New Year's?
This year is going to be uplifting!

Why are New Year's kisses so special?

They're sealed with the year's first love.

What do you call someone who stays up past midnight on New Year's Eve?

A dreamer!

Why doesn't Santa like taking selfies?

He prefers his "elfies."

What do you get if you eat Christmas decorations?

Tinsellitis!

Why did the ornament go to therapy?

It felt like it was hanging by a thread.

What does a gingerbread man use to keep warm?

A cookie sheet.

Why did Santa's workshop hire a comedian?

To keep the elves in high spirits.

What did one reindeer say to another?

I sleigh, you sleigh, we all sleigh!

What's Frosty's favorite breakfast?

Snowflakes.

Why don't elves play chess?
They're afraid of the knight.

What do you call an elf who sings?
A wrapper.

Why did the snowman go to college?
To become a cool scholar.

What's Santa's favorite weather?
It's rain-deer!

Why did the mistletoe break up with the Christmas tree?
It felt like it wasn't getting enough attention.

How do sheep wish each other Merry Christmas?
Fleece Navidad.

What do elves do after school?

Their gnome-work.

Why was the reindeer embarrassed?

It saw its reflection and thought it looked Rudolph-ulous.

What's a penguin's favorite part of Christmas dinner?

The ice-cream pudding.

Why doesn't Santa eat at fancy
restaurants?
Because he has elf-care.

What does Santa say when taking
attendance at the North Pole?
Present!

What's a Christmas tree's least
favorite accessory?
The topper–it's always at a point.

Why did Santa bring a ladder?
To reach the high spirits.

What do you call a reindeer with bad manners?
Rude-olph.

Why are Christmas trees such bad knitters?
They drop needles.

What did the snowman order at the diner?
An ice burger.

Why did the elf sit on the shelf?
It wanted to be above the rest.

What's a snowman's favorite school subject?
Chill-ogy.

Why was the snowman looking through the carrots?
He was picking his nose!

What do you call Santa when he's taking a break?
Santa Pause.

Why did the elf go to school?
To improve his elf-esteem.

What do you get when you cross a
snowman with a dog?
Frostbite.

Why do Christmas trees like to knit?
Because they love needles.

What's a snowman's favorite drink?
Iced tea.

How does a snowman get around?

By riding an icicle.

Why does Santa have three gardens?

So he can ho ho ho.

What do you call a greedy elf?

Elfish.

What kind of music do elves like best?
Wrap music.

What do snowmen eat for breakfast?
Frosted flakes.

What is the Christmas tree's favorite candy?
Ornamints.

Why did Rudolph never get a good report card?
Because he went down in history!

What do you get if you cross a bell with a skunk?
Jingle smells.

Why don't penguins like talking?
Because they find it ice-breaking.

What's Santa's favorite kind of potato chip?
Kringle-cut.

Why was the ornament feeling low?
It felt like it wasn't hanging right.

Why don't Christmas trees sew?
They keep dropping their needles.

How do snowmen greet each other?

Ice to meet you!

Why did Santa go to music school?

To improve his wrapping skills.

What do you call a reindeer that tells jokes?

A comedian-deer.

Why did the candy cane break up with the peppermint?

It found them too sweet.

What's a reindeer's favorite game?

Truth or deer.

Why don't elves ever get arrested?

They have high elf-esteem.

What's a Christmas tree's least
favorite thing?
Getting lit.

What did one Christmas light say to
the other?
You light up my life.

What's an elf's favorite dessert?
Shortbread.

Why do snowmen hate summer?
It's a total meltdown.

How do you lift a frozen car?
With a jack frost.

What do you call Santa if he loses his pants?
St. Nicker-less.

Why did the calendar start a diet?
It wanted to turn over a new leaf.

Why was the clock excited for New Year's Eve?
It was ready to have a ball.

What do you call a ghost's New Year's party?
Boo Year's Eve.

Why do calendars love January 1st?

It's a fresh start.

What's a bee's favorite way to celebrate New Year's?

With a buzz.

Why don't calendars ever get tired?

They're always refreshed every year.

What did the champagne glass say to
the bottle?
You pop my cork!

What do you call someone who makes
resolutions but never keeps them?
A new fear resolutionist.

Why did the baby celebrate New
Year's?
It's their birthday!

What's a New Year's baby's favorite sport?
Kick-off.

Why did the elevator love New Year's?
It was ready to go up.

What do cows say on New Year's Eve?
Moo Year!

Why do phones enjoy New Year's Eve?

They get a fresh restart.

What do vampires do on New Year's Eve?

Count down.

What's a snake's New Year's resolution?

To hiss less.

Why did the fireworks blush?
They saw sparks flying.

What's the best way to start the New Year?
With a clean slate.

Why do gym memberships spike in January?
New Year, new me.

Why don't you argue with New Year's resolutions?

They're always right on time.

What's the most common New Year's resolution?

1080p vision.

What do you call a snowman with a six-pack?

An abdominal snowman.

Why was Santa's helper so stressed?

He had too much "elf" work.

Why don't snowmen ever argue?

They just let it go.

What did Mrs. Claus say when Santa asked her the weather?

It looks like rain, dear.

Why does Santa never get a parking ticket?

He parks on the roof.

What's an elf's favorite part of the school day?

The present-ation.

Why was the Christmas tree at the dentist?

It needed a root canal.

What's Santa's favorite exercise?

Ho-Ho-Ho-lates.

What's a reindeer's favorite genre of music?

Wrap.

What do you get if you cross Santa with a detective?

Santa Clues.

Why do elves love playing in the snow?

They're natural flakes.

What did the snowman say to the robin?

I'm snow glad to see you!

Why did the gingerbread man feel bad?

He was crumbling under the pressure.

What do you call Santa when he loses
his memory?
Forgetta Claus.

Why did the elf go to the bank?
To check his snow-balance.

What do you call a cat on Christmas?
Santa Claws.

Why don't reindeer ever get lost?
They follow their noses.

What did the marshmallow say at the
Christmas party?
I'm feeling toasty.

Why do bells make great friends?
They're always ringing in.

What's a snowman's favorite kind of cake?

Carrot cake.

What do you call a reindeer that loves math?

Rudolph the Red-Nosed Remainder.

Why did the elf bring a ladder to the party?

To get to new heights.

What do you call a Christmas gift that sings?

A wrap star.

Why did Santa cancel his vacation?

He needed to sleigh at work.

What do elves use to clean their hands?

Santatizer.

Why was the fireplace embarrassed?
It saw Santa in his Claus-tume.

What's Frosty's favorite drink at the bar?
Snow cones.

How do Christmas angels greet each other?
Halo!

What did the Christmas card say to
the stamp?

Stick with me, and we'll go places.

Why did the reindeer bring a map?

It didn't want to get sleigh-ted.

Why was the turkey invited to the
band?

It had drumsticks.

What's Santa's favorite type of bagel?

Jingle bagels.

What do you call a train loaded with candy?

A sweet toot!

What do you call Frosty in the morning?

A puddle.

Why did Santa break up with Mrs. Claus?

She sleighed his heart.

Why do snow globes make great friends?

They're well-rounded.

What's an elf's favorite vegetable?

Celery-because it's "elfy!"

Why did the polar bear wear a scarf?
It was feeling a little frosty.

What do Santa's helpers learn in school?
The elf-abet.

What's the Christmas tree's favorite hobby?
Branching out.

Why was the reindeer worried about school?

It was afraid of failing its sleigh-bell test.

What's Santa's favorite video game?

SleighStation.

What did the Christmas ornament say to the tree?

I find you very appealing.

Why did Santa go to the doctor?
He was feeling Claus-trophobic.

What do you call Santa's laundry detergent?
Yule Tide.

What did Santa say when he accidentally left a present?
Oh, snap!

Why did the elf buy a ladder?
To reach the Christmas spirit.

Why does Rudolph always look great?
He uses lots of "deer" products.

What's an elf's favorite candy?
Jolly Ranchers.

Why did Frosty the Snowman call his friends?

He wanted to have a snow-ball.

What do elves wear on their feet?

Mistletoes.

Why did the snowman refuse dessert?

He was stuffed with ice cream.

Why don't elves ever retire?
They love their job and won't shelf themselves.

What's Santa's favorite mode of transportation?
A sleigh-cycle.

What do you call Santa's cousins?
Relative Claus.

What do reindeer hang on their
Christmas trees?
Horn-aments.

What do you call a snowman's dog?
Slush Puppy.

What do elves do to exercise?
Jingle bell squats.

Why was Santa late for work?

He got snowed in.

What's a snowman's favorite pet?

A snowshoe hare.

Why do firecrackers love New Year's Eve?

Because they like to make a bang!

What's the best way to pay for a New Year's resolution?
With change.

Why did the clock throw a party?
To make time fly.

What's a chicken's favorite way to celebrate New Year's?
With a cluck countdown.

Why was the New Year's Day parade
so windy?

Because it was full of hot air!

Why did the scarecrow celebrate New
Year's?

It wanted to turn over a new leaf.

What do you call New Year's
fireworks that don't go off?

A missed spark.

What did the calendar say on January 1st?

It's about time!

Why do mathematicians love New Year's Eve?

They love the countdown.

What's a frog's New Year's resolution?

To leap into action!

Why don't eggs make New Year's resolutions?

They crack under pressure.

What did the New Year's toast say to the butter?

Let's start this year on a roll.

What's the best way to celebrate New Year's at sea?

With a wave.

Why did the broom love New Year's Eve?

It swept away the old year.

What's a horse's favorite New Year's song?

Auld Hay Syne.

Why did the grape stop partying on New Year's Eve?

It ran out of juice.

What did the clock say to the
hourglass at midnight?
Time's up!

What's a cat's New Year's resolution?
To purr more, hiss less.

Why did the party hat go to school?
**It wanted to be the life of the
classroom.**

What's a New Year's resolution that always gets broken?
A gym membership.

Why was the pencil excited for New Year's Eve?
It was ready to draw new beginnings.

What do you call a crab that celebrates New Year's?
A shell-ebration!

Why do people celebrate New Year's with champagne?
Because it's pop-tastic!

What do clocks say on New Year's Day?
Tick-tock, let's rock!

Why did the man throw a clock out the window on New Year's Eve?
To see time fly!

Why was the gym so crowded on January 2nd?

Everyone was working out their resolutions.

What's the best New Year's treat?

Countdown cookies.

Why did the computer celebrate New Year's?

It wanted to refresh.

What's a dog's New Year's resolution?

To paw-sitively chase more fun.

Why do we drop a ball on New Year's Eve?

Because it's the best way to let things fall into place.

Why was the balloon so happy on New Year's Eve?

It wanted to pop into the new year.

What's a clock's favorite game on
New Year's?
Tic-Tock-Toe.

What's a banana's New Year's
resolution?
To stop peeling under pressure.

Why do people write New Year's
resolutions in pencil?
So they can erase them!

What's the best way to end the old year?
With a smile and a toast.

What do you call a group of cows celebrating New Year's?
Moo Year's Eve.

Why don't calendars get tired?
They stay refreshed every year.

What's a pirate's favorite way to celebrate New Year's?

Arrr-angements for the party!

Why do resolutions fail?

Because they're made on tired promises.

What did the bubble say on New Year's Eve?

Let's pop into the next year.

What's the easiest resolution to keep?
Watching the clock!

Why do stars love New Year's?
It's their time to shine.

What do firecrackers eat for New Year's dinner?
Spark-tatoes.

Why did the thermometer get invited
to the New Year's party?
It was hot stuff.

What's a skunk's New Year's wish?
A scent-sational year ahead.

What's a ghost's favorite countdown
phrase?
Boo-year, boo-year!

Why was the mirror excited for New Year's?

It wanted to reflect on the past.

What do chefs say on New Year's Day?

Lettuce celebrate!

Why was the fish excited for New Year's?

It wanted to scale up.

What do clouds say on New Year's Day?

Let's clear the air.

What's the best way to handle mistakes from the old year?

With grace and a new start.

Why was the light bulb excited for January?

It saw a bright year ahead.

What's the favorite drink of New
Year's Eve parties?
Fizz-tastic cocktails.

Why did the candy cane stay up late?
To stick around for the countdown.

What's the best thing to say at
midnight on New Year's?
Cheers to new beginnings!

Why do shoes celebrate New Year's?
They want to kick off the new year right.

What's a baker's favorite New Year's resolution?
To rise to the occasion.

Why do fans love New Year's parties?
They blow everyone away.

What do party hats say on January 1st?

Let's top this year!

Why was the stopwatch invited to New Year's?

It wanted to count every second.

Why did the rainbow celebrate New Year's?

It wanted a colorful start.

What's a flower's New Year's resolution?
To bloom where it's planted.

Why did the toast become a motivational speaker?
It wanted to spread positivity.

What's the best way to organize New Year's resolutions?
With bullet points.

Why did the cup of coffee stay up till midnight?

It wanted to espresso its feelings.

What's the favorite shape of New Year's decorations?

Round–they symbolize unity and completeness.

Why was the soda can excited for New Year's?

It wanted to pop open the fun.

What's a firefighter's favorite New Year's Eve activity?
Watching sparks fly.

Why do frogs throw parties on New Year's?
To make it ribbiting.

Why did the star love New Year's Eve?
It wanted to shine the brightest.

Why did Rudolph never get a good report card?
Because he went down in history!

What do you get if you cross a bell with a skunk?
Jingle smells.

Why don't penguins like talking?
Because they find it ice-breaking.

What's Santa's favorite kind of potato chip?
Kringle-cut.

Why was the ornament feeling low?
It felt like it wasn't hanging right.

How do snowmen greet each other?
Ice to meet you!

Why did Santa go to music school?
To improve his wrapping skills.

What do you call a reindeer that tells jokes?
A comedian-deer.

Why did the candy cane break up with the peppermint?
It found them too sweet.

What's a reindeer's favorite game?
Truth or deer.

Why don't elves ever get arrested?
They have high elf-esteem.

What's a Christmas tree's least
favorite thing?
Getting lit.

What did one Christmas light say to
the other?
You light up my life.

What's an elf's favorite dessert?
Shortbread.

Why do snowmen hate summer?
It's a total meltdown.

How do you lift a frozen car?
With a jack frost.

What do you call Santa if he loses his
pants?
St. Nicker-less.

What did the champagne glass say to
the bottle?
You pop my cork!

THANK YOU!